MINDFUL MASTERY IN THE MIDST OF MAYHEM

10 Practical Ways for Busy Professionals to Benefit from Mindfulness Despite a Packed Schedule

J Paloma Litteral

J Litteral

ISBN: 9798878359726

Cover design by: Art Painter
Library of Congress Control Number: 2018675309
Printed in the United States of America

CONTENTS

AUTHOR'S NOTE

Firstly, thank you so much for making a little investment in yourself. I'm sure that if you apply what you find in this book, you'll yield a much higher return.

I am Paloma, a former work-aholic. For many years, I used work as an escape from the threatening reality of my own emotions.Sadly, I wasn't alone in this.

Thankfully, I've learned and honed many skills that have enabled me to better balance my inner and outer worlds. Mindfulness was key to this process, even though I didn't know its name at the time.

This book has intentionally been kept short and direct, with simple wording and lots of "silly" and "cliché" illustrations. The idea is to make it so easy to read and apply that it doesn't create any resistance.

My sincere hope is that this book empowers you to gain new perspectives about and actively apply many things you probably already know.

May you find exactly what you need to create the enjoyment you deserve to experience in life.

Paloma

INTRODUCTION

In the bustling cityscape of our lives, picture Alex, a young professional, anxiously darting through crowded streets, phone buzzing, deadlines looming, and a never-ending to-do list.

The rhythm of urban chaos plays as the soundtrack to Alex's day, leaving little room for peace.

Yet, amidst this whirlwind, there's a tool, a beacon of calmness. What is it? Mindfulness.

Imagine the city as a symphony of honks, footsteps, and ringing phones, each demanding attention, leaving Alex feeling like a tiny boat in a vast and stormy sea.

Alex's story echoes the daily reality for many of us. Yet, through the jarring racket of demands, mindfulness emerges as a lighthouse—a guide to navigate the tumultuous waters of a hectic life.

What is Mindfulness?

Being Fully Present in the Moment

Imagine your mind as a spotlight. Mindfulness is like adjusting that spotlight to shine on the current moment, whether it's tackling a work project or enjoying a warm cup of tea.

It's like when you're reading a thrilling book, and you're so engrossed in the story that the rest of the world fades away. Mindfulness is bringing that kind of focus to everything you do.

Mindfulness is an ancient practice, like an old, wise friend who's been around the block. In the historical record, it's most associated with Eastern traditions where many attempted to incorporate the power of being fully present in their daily lives.

We might think of it as an ancient recipe for tranquility. Passed down through generations, it's a mix of wisdom and experience, making it timeless.

It's a Proven Technique

Even a brief review of some of the research about mindfulness shows us what a valuable tool it is.

Although it seems "too good to be true" because of its simplicity, the positive effects are far-reaching. Studies have shown improvements in everything from blood pressure and sleep to depression and anxiety.

It's certainly not a cure. However, it's one powerful piece of a successful approach to difficulties more and more people face.

Handling Stress with a Shield: Mindfulness won't erase the challenges, but it equips you with a shield, helping you face stress with resilience.

Picture stress as a storm. Mindfulness provides an umbrella, not to stop the rain but to help you walk through it without getting drenched.

Mindfulness isn't just about the mind; it's a tonic for the heart. It nurtures emotional well-being, fostering a sense of calm amidst life's storms.

Imagine emotions as waves. We don't ignore the waves. We don't fight them or try to change their nature. Mindfulness is learning to surf, riding the highs and lows with grace and balance.

Closing Thoughts

As we embark on this journey together, we'll uncover practical mindfulness tools tailored for the busiest professionals.

Like planting seeds of calm amidst the chaos, these practices are invitations to pause, breathe, and reclaim control.

As someone with a full schedule, you may feel overwhelmed by the thought of applying everything all at once.

Please do not add even more pressure to your life. Although the practices are simple and the chapters are intentionally short, it may not be brainless to add this into your schedule.

It may be most beneficial to simply add a reminder to read one chapter each week. Practice the technique with a view to finding the best way to fit it into your life.

There are no right or wrong answers here. It's simply a learning experience.

Join me in exploring the art of mindful mastery, a guide to finding serenity even in the busiest cityscapes of life.

Important Note

It is crucial that you take charge of your own well-being. Please do not rely on any single outside source for decisions as weighty as those related to your health, mentally, emotionally, or physically.

At the end of this book are resources I've found helpful and that you might consider in doing your own research. Although I am a highly trained coach, I am not a licensed medical or psychiatric professional.
If you need any immediate assistance, please contact emergency services. You may also contact a hotline in your country.

Always consult your own healthcare professionals for the best guidance.

CHAPTER 1: UTILIZE THE POWER OF BREATH

Regardless of how hectic life becomes, our breath remains a constant companion—a reliable guide back to the present moment.

Exploring the Link Between Breath and Mindfulness

Your breath is akin to a gentle wave, a rhythm that grounds you in the present.

Picture your breath as the soothing waves on a calm beach, offering a natural connection to the now.

Mindfulness elevates your breath to a starring role, a conduit to the essence of each passing moment.

The Calming Impact of Mindful Breathing

Observing your breath opens a secret door to a tranquil garden amid life's chaos.

Do your best to remember to take a deep breath during moments of anxiety—a superhero move rescuing you from stress.

Mindful breathing signals to your body and mind that it's okay to slow down, creating a bubble of calmness amidst life's storm.

4-7-8 Breathing Technique

The 4-7-8 technique is one highly impactful technique for calming the storm within, adaptable to any situation.

1. Inhale quietly through your nose for a count of 4.
2. Hold your breath for a count of 7.
3. Exhale completely through your mouth for a count of 8.

Envision inflating and deflating a balloon—a rhythmic pattern tapping into the calming power of your breath.

There is no special magic in the specific numbers of 4-7-8. Experiment with different lengths of time, holding between the inhale and exhale.

You may also find adding a hold between the exhale and inhale relaxing as well.

Here are a few other timings you might try:

1. Box Breathing: 4 seconds per inhale - hold - exhale - hold
2. Alternate 8-5: 8 seconds per inhale and exhale, 5 seconds per hold
3. Extended Box Breathing: 10 seconds per each inhale, exhale, and hold

Make this technique even more powerful by simultaneously intensely focusing on a simple and positive thought: relaxing on the beach, laughing with loved ones, being told you got a raise, or that first sip of coffee.

Incorporating the Technique into Daily Routines

The simplicity and versatility of these kinds of breathing

practices make them a seamless addition to your daily activities.

Integrate the technique during moments of waiting or brief pauses in your day—a mini-vacation for your mind.

By making this technique a part of your routine, you're not merely managing stress; you're enhancing your overall well-being—a miniscule investment for a significantly large return.

Closing Thoughts

Breath awareness is your passport to the present—a journey toward peace and serenity.

In the chapters ahead, I encourage you to layer the other exercises with awareness of your breath. This creates a path to a centered and serene you.

Please give yourself permission to go at your own pace and experiment with one technique at a time. Simply becoming aware of your current breathing habits is a fantastic start.

CHAPTER 2: THE ART OF MINDFUL OBSERVATION

In the colorful canvas of our lives, we often rush past the details, missing the subtle brushstrokes that paint the world around us.

What if I told you that the power to unlock clarity, presence, and a deeper connection with your surroundings lies in the simple act of observation?

Welcome to The Art of Mindful Observation—a chapter that unfolds like a journey through an art gallery, where every detail tells a story.

The Power of Observation

Observation is more than just physically seeing with the eyes. It's about opening your senses to the rich tapestry of the present moment.

Imagine you're in a garden. Observation is not just seeing the flowers; it's inhaling their fragrance, feeling the texture of the petals, and listening to the gentle rustle of leaves.

Observation in Mindfulness

Mindful observation is the lens through which we perceive the world without the filters such as those of judgments or preconceived notions.

We might liken it to wiping clean the foggy window of your mind, allowing the clarity of the present to shine through.

Benefits of Cultivating a Non-Judgmental Awareness

Cultivating non-judgmental awareness through observation opens a gateway to a more profound understanding of yourself and the world around you.

Reflect on a time when a coworker's actions seemed puzzling. What if we actually saw them as a puzzle, a complex set of diverse pieces?

Observation without judgment allows you to explore the pieces without immediately trying to force them into a predetermined picture.

Enhanced Self-Understanding: Observation without judgment lets you explore your thoughts and emotions without criticism.

Improved Relationships: Non-judgmental observation in interactions fosters empathy and deepens connections.

Five Senses Check-In

The Five Senses Check-In is your passport to the world of mindful observation. It's a practice that engages each sense intentionally, allowing you to savor the richness of your surroundings.

Engaging Each Sense Mindfully

Sight: Observe the colors, shapes, and details around you. Notice the interplay of light and shadow.

Hearing: Tune into the soundscape—whether it's the hum of the city or the rustle of leaves in a quiet park.

Touch: Feel the textures beneath your fingertips, whether it's the smooth surface of a desk or the rough bark of a tree.

Smell: Inhale deeply and identify the various scents in your environment. Let each breath be a connection to the present.

Taste: The next time you eat or drink, savor the flavors in your mouth. Even a simple sip of water can become a mindful experience.

Adapting the Practice to Various Environments

Our first instinct is likely that this type of quiet observation is only for specific places. The reality is, it's useful in any environment.

In a bustling office, observe the hum of activity—keyboard clicks, distant conversations, and the rhythm of footsteps.

While attending an online meeting, take stock of your virtual environment. Take a moment to observe the software's capabilities, the facial expressions of the presenter, or the telling details of a speaker's background.

Each sense check-in can be tailored to fit the unique environment you find yourself in.

The beauty of the Five Senses Check-In is its adaptability. Whether you're in a crowded subway or a quiet park, you can always find a moment for mindful observation.

It doesn't have to take long, even just 30 seconds is enough to help you refocus on the present moment. Often, this can reduce the volume of the many "what if" thoughts that plague us, perhaps silencing them all together.

Closing Thoughts

We've had a glimpse into the power that lies in truly seeing, hearing, touching, smelling, and tasting the world around us.

As we continue this journey, remember that observation is not a passive act; it's an active engagement with the richness of each moment.

In the upcoming chapters, we'll explore more ways to infuse mindfulness into various aspects of our lives.

So, let's open our senses to the symphony of life, observe without judgment, and uncover the beauty that awaits in the ordinary moments of our extraordinary lives.

CHAPTER 3: MAGNIFICENT MINDFUL MICRO-BREAKS

For the majority of us, it is all too easy to get swept away by the unending flow of tasks. Each one seems to urgently call out for completion.

What if I told you that taking a step back, even for just a minute, could actually be a key to unlocking both increased productivity and well-being?

Let's dive into the surprising effects of the micro-break—a short, sweet pause that holds the power to rejuvenate your mind in the midst of chaos.

Recognizing the Need for Breaks

Life's demands can be like a never-ending race, leaving us breathless and drained.

Imagine running a marathon without a single water break. It's not sustainable. Our minds, much like our bodies, need moments to recharge.

These don't have to be long or dramatic, just a little strategic.

Continuous Work on Productivity Takes a Toll

Contrary to the belief that non-stop work leads to peak productivity, it often results in burnout and decreased efficiency instead.

We often compare our computers to our brains, and with good reason. Without regular breaks, our computers can overheat, slowing down and impacting overall performance.

Our biological ultra-computers (our brains) experience comparable consequences.

The simplicity of a mindful micro-break provides a much needed reprieve and offers a mini-reset.

These aren't just ordinary breaks. They're like little miracles sprinkled throughout your day, bringing moments of clarity and calm.

One-Minute Mindful Pause

A simple yet profound technique for a quick mental reset.

1. Find or create a quiet spot.
2. Close your eyes and take a slow deep breath.
3. Imagine that you can literally inhale positivity and exhale tension.
4. Repeat this a few times.
5. Open your eyes, refocused and recharged.

It's like pressing a reset button for your mind, creating space for renewed focus.

Does it last forever? Of course not.

Does it help? Absolutely. Every little bit helps and it has a cumulative effect.

Integrating Micro-Breaks into a Busy Schedule

Mindful micro-breaks don't require elaborate rituals. Here are a few additional simple exercises to try:

Shoulder rolls, neck stretches, or a quick mindfulness mantra—these exercises take only a minute but can make a world of difference.

You don't need to clear your schedule; you can seamlessly weave these breaks into your existing routine.

This is where a little strategy is needed.

Instead of scrolling through your phone during a short break, try a one-minute mindful pause.

Continuing to perform tasks that require layers of micro-decisions is not a break. You pour a lot of data into your brain during a few hours at work. It's simultaneously quite busy making decisions.

If you're feeling tired, overwhelmed, or uncertain, your brain might be saying, "Hey! Please give me a break."

Just one to five minutes of pausing and reflecting on the present moment can have quite an effect. This shift is similar to adjusting your focus to view another perspective of an optical illusion.

It's a minimal investment in your mental well-being that pays high dividends throughout the day.

Closing Thoughts

As you give it a try, remember that taking a moment for yourself isn't a luxury; it's a necessity.

In the upcoming chapters, we'll explore more of these pocket-sized mindfulness practices, each a small but mighty tool to navigate the bustling landscape of your daily life.

For now, let's embrace the power of the micro-break, discovering the tranquility that lies in the spaces between the chaos.

CHAPTER 4: EMBRACING MINDFUL GRATITUDE

Gratitude might seem like a distant or "woo-y" concept.

What if I told you that cultivating gratitude isn't just a feel-good notion; it's a powerful tool that can transform your perspective, alleviate stress, and enhance your overall well-being?

We'll explore mindful gratitude—a practice that invites you to focus on the beauty in the ordinary and the joy in the everyday.

Cultivating Gratitude in Daily Life

Life often moves at such a rapid pace that it often leaves little room for appreciation.

As a business professional, how do you feel if your efforts and achievements are not recognized?

How long would you stay at an organization that overlooked all the good you do?

You could be the owner with customers who leave negative reviews or an entry-level employee whose boss largely ignores you, it's a recipe for disaster.

Exploring the Psychological Benefits of Gratitude

Gratitude is more than a polite "thank you"; it's a mental and emotional tonic.

In the world of business, it's money. Customer loyalty is motivated by gratitude.

As individuals, gratitude invests in positive thoughts, allowing them to grow and flourish.

The Impact of Gratitude on Stress and Well-being

The practice of gratitude acts as a shield against stress, creating a ripple effect on your overall well-being.

Gratitude empowers you to navigate life's storms with a sense of calm.

Gratitude Journaling

Keeping a record of things you're grateful for is like appreciation fertilizer for your gratitude garden.

1. Set aside a few minutes each day.
2. Reflect on the positive aspects of your day.
3. Write down brief notes in your gratitude journal.

It's like creating a portfolio of positivity, highlighting the moments that bring a smile to your face.

Establishing a Daily Gratitude Practice

Making gratitude a habit requires consistency and commitment.

Just like watering a plant every day helps it grow, daily gratitude journaling nurtures a positive mindset.

If writing in a paper journal isn't for you, don't worry. There are plenty of other options:

- Online / PDF journal
- Message / email yourself
- Artistic journals with sketches or drawings
- A brief note in your planner / online calendar
- Sharing your list with a loved one

Choose a specific time, perhaps before bed or during your morning coffee, to reflect on three things you're grateful for.

It's another small investment with profound returns.

Challenges may arise, but perseverance is the key to reaping the benefits of gratitude.

Think of it as nurturing a partnership. Sometimes it requires effort, but the bond grows stronger over time.

If you miss a day, don't be discouraged. Like any practice, consistency is a journey, not a destination.

Closing Thoughts

Remember that gratitude isn't about ignoring life's challenges but about shifting your focus to the positive aspects.

In the chapters ahead, we'll delve into more mindful practices, several of which utilize the practice of inviting gratitude into your life.

Why not take a moment now to embrace the beauty in the ordinary, cultivate gratitude, and watch as it transforms our daily experiences into moments of joy and appreciation?

CHAPTER 5: NAVIGATING THE DIGITAL LANDSCAPE MINDFULLY

Having become a daily norm for most, technology is a double-edged sword—it connects us, entertains us, but can also pull us into a whirlpool of constant connectivity.

In this chapter, we'll explore the delicate dance between technology and mindfulness, discovering how to use our devices without letting them dictate our lives.

The Relationship Between Technology and Mindfulness

Technology is woven into the fabric of our daily existence, shaping how we communicate, work, and unwind.

Imagine your smartphone as a literal blade. It could be used as a sword, a weapon for destruction, or a farming implement, a tool for growth. We must learn to wield it with caution and intent.

Pitfalls of Constant Connectivity

The constant barrage of notifications and updates can be overwhelming, leading to a state of perpetual anxiety and distraction.

Picture a constant stream of messages as a swarm of bees

buzzing around you.

It's hard to focus on anything else when you're constantly tense and either trying to ignore them or swatting them away.

The Need for Mindful Tech Use

Mindful technology use is about taking control, being intentional, and using these tools to enhance our lives, not control them.

Just like a master pianist doesn't let the piano keys dictate the melody, we shouldn't let technology dictate our lives.

Create Designated Periods for Digital Detox

Set aside specific times when you intentionally disconnect from your devices.

You're right, this practice can be downright painful. Let's be honest, we've become attached to, dependent upon, and addicted to these devices.

What better reason for occasional detoxes to regain control?

Consider designating an hour before bedtime as a tech-free zone, allowing your mind to unwind without the distraction of screens.

Establishing Boundaries for a Healthier Relationship with Technology

Boundaries are the guardrails that keep us on the path of mindful tech use.

Think of it as building a fence around a garden. It keeps what's valuable inside and protects it from external threats.

Establish a "no-phone zone" during meals to savor the flavors without digital distractions. This simple practice fosters a healthier relationship with technology.

Closing Thoughts

In our journey through the digital landscape, we do well to remember that technology is a tool, not a master. By using it mindfully, we can harness its benefits without succumbing to its pitfalls.

As we move into the second half of the book, consider how technology has supported or hindered your application of the previous practices.

How will you use this data to create a more empowering strategy for the chapters to come?

CHAPTER 6: THE DANCE OF MINDFUL MOVEMENT

In the rhythm of our busy lives, movement often takes a backseat.

What if I told you that incorporating mindful movement into your day isn't just about staying physically active—it's a dance that harmonizes the body and mind?

Let's get into the groove of mindful movement, where every step, stretch, and sway becomes a choreography of well-being.

Incorporating Movement into Mindfulness

Movement isn't just about exercise; it's a bridge to mindfulness, connecting our physical and mental selves.

For millennia, we humans have used it to communicate, to stay safe, and to explore our emotional side.

Each of these requires being focused on the moment to achieve the desired targets.

Physical activity is known for its power to uplift your mood and clear the mental fog.

Think of a brisk walk as opening a window on a stuffy day —it lets in fresh air, rejuvenating both your body and mind.

Accessible Movement Practices for Busy Professionals

Even in the busiest of schedules, there's room for mindful movement.

You don't need a gym membership or hours of free time. Mindful movement is about weaving it seamlessly into your existing routine.

Take the stairs instead of the elevator or have a walking meeting.

Walk in place or dance around while you're on hold, watching a video, or waiting for your next client.

Consider switching to a standing desk or a stability ball instead of a cushy office chair.

These small adjustments accumulate into a dance of daily activity.

Desk Yoga

Bringing the serenity of yoga to your workspace with simple yoga stretches for the office.

Remember to only do these poses if it's safe for you and to do them slowly and carefully. Consult your healthcare professional for the best guidance.

Seated Cat-Cow: Inhale slowly as you push your ribs forward and round your spine while you look up. Exhale and arch your back like a cat as you tuck your chin.

Chair Pigeon Pose: Cross one ankle over the opposite knee, feeling a gentle stretch.

Desk Forward Fold: Stand away from your desk and hinge at your hips, reaching for your desk to stretch your back and hamstrings.

Benefits of Integrating Mindful Movement into the Workday

Enhances Focus: Mindful movement acts like a mental reset, sharpening your focus.

Stress Reduction: These simple stretches release tension, creating a sense of calm.

Boosts Energy: Movement stimulates blood flow, revitalizing your body and mind.

Closing Thoughts

In this chapter of mindful movement, we've explored the poetry of motion—the way it intertwines with mindfulness to create a symphony of well-being.

As we continue this journey, remember that movement isn't a chore; it's a celebration of what your body and mind can achieve together.

Next, we'll continue to explore more ways to infuse mindfulness into every step, making the dance of well-being a seamless part of your daily routine.

Keep moving, keep dancing, and discover the joy that mindful movement brings to the intricate melody of our lives.

CHAPTER 7: YOUR TICKET TO THE MINDFUL LISTENING CONCERT

If listening were a concert, each word would be a note and every pause an opportunity to connect deeply with the audience.

Next, let's unravel the importance of active listening with the objectives of mindful communication. To that end, we'll explore how reflective listening can transform conversations in a professional setting.

Importance of Active Listening

Listening is more than simply hearing the sounds we call speech. It requires understanding the underlying melody.

Imagine a conversation as a musical piece. Without attentive listening, you might miss the subtle nuances—the emotions, concerns, and the unsaid notes that linger.

This is what your mom was talking about when she said, "Do you think I just like hearing myself talk?" She wanted you to actively listen, just as you want your employees to listen to you.

Question for meditation: What kind of listener am I?

Mindful listening is the glue that binds relationships: fostering understanding and trust, demonstrating empathy and responsiveness, and creating a harmonious connection.

Barriers to Effective Listening in a Professional Setting

Despite its importance, barriers often hinder effective listening in professional environments.

These barriers can be like an unstable streaming connection, disrupting the clarity of the message being conveyed.

Distractions, preconceived notions, and the pressure of a busy schedule often prevent us from fully loading the "song" the other person is offering.

Reflective Listening

Reflective listening is a key to unlocking the full potential of mindful communication. As we review some techniques and examples, consider which you're already using and which would be beneficial to implement.

Paraphrasing: Repeat what you heard in your own words to confirm understanding.

"If I understand correctly, you feel our time would be better spent on this instead of that."

Clarifying: Ask questions for clarity rather than making assumptions.

"Could you give me an example to help me see what that might look like in practical terms?"

Empathizing: Acknowledge and validate the speaker's

emotions.

"I can understand why you would feel frustrated with the situation."

It is extremely important to clarify that empathizing is not the same as condoning or agreeing. In some cases, it may be necessary to clarify this.

"I understand why the situation would cause you to feel frustrated. ...

If you're the boss: *"... It's also critical that we calmly and respectfully work towards finding a solution. Do you need a minute to calm down?"*

If you are peers or a subordinate: *"... My experience has been different but I absolutely support finding a beneficial solution."*

When and how this is most appropriate will become more obvious if we're mindfully present and paying attention to the "now" more than our worry.

Summarizing: Recap the key points to show you've grasped the message.

"I will make a note that you've pushed back the launch by three weeks due to a technical glitch that's already being resolved."

To be frank, this type of listening is not always easy. However, it has multiple benefits, many of which we've already covered. Let's look at one more you may not have considered.

Reflective listening is like holding up a mirror to the speaker's thoughts, allowing him to see his ideas more clearly and creating an opportunity to correct any misunderstandings.

Despite the initial extra investment of patience and time, my experience has taught me that mindful listening is priceless.

Closing Thoughts

In short, listening mindfully deeply impacts our professional relationships.

As we continue this journey, remember that listening is not the same as hearing—it's an active engagement with the thoughts and feelings of others.

Examine what happens as you embrace the art of listening, cultivate empathy, and witness how the simple act of attentive hearing can transform our professional landscapes into harmonious collaborations.

Next, we'll turn our listening skills inward as we learn to answer the call for food.

CHAPTER 8: DIGESTING THE CONCEPT OF MINDFUL EATING

With overflowing daily schedules, meals often become just another task to simply check off the to-do list.

What if I told you that each bite is an opportunity for a mindful experience, a chance to savor the flavors and appreciate the nourishment your food brings?

Let's bite into the practice of mindful eating, where every meal becomes a time capsule back to the present moment.

Mindfulness and Eating Habits

Mindful eating isn't just about what you eat; it's about how you eat. It's an awareness that transforms meals into moments of joy.

Imagine your meal as a piece of art. Mindful eating is like studying each brushstroke, appreciating the colors and textures that make each bite a masterpiece.

Mindful eating is bringing your full attention to the present moment, embracing a deeper connection with your food.

It's like turning the volume up on a favorite song—you

don't just hear the music; you feel it, resonating with it as each note plays.

Benefits of Savoring and Appreciating Food

Beyond nutrition, mindful eating enhances the pleasure and satisfaction derived from meals.

Honestly, this one is a challenge for me as I've had a rocky relationship with food. I know I'm not alone and maybe you're in the same boat.

"Why do I need to enjoy it? It's just eating."

The truth is, mindful eating does a lot more than make us happy.

Improved Digestion: When you savor each bite, your body has the time and energy it needs to orchestrate efficient digestion.

Healthy Weight Management: Mindful eating reduces the tendency to overeat by fostering awareness of hunger and fullness.

Making each meal a mindful experience doesn't require a complete overhaul. It's about small, intentional steps.

Pause Before Eating: Take a moment to appreciate your meal visually before taking the first bite.

Engage Your Senses: Notice the aroma, colors, and textures. Feel the temperature of your food.

Chew Slowly and Enjoy: Instead of rushing, savor each bite. It's a journey, not a race.

Overcoming Common Challenges

For hard workers like you, finding time for a leisurely meal might seem challenging.

Start by choosing one meal a day for mindful eating, gradually expanding as it becomes a natural part of your routine.

It's more important to build a habit than to be a champion at it. Choose the meal that would be easiest for you to eat at a slower pace.

If that means starting with the smallest meal, a snack, or even just part of a meal, that's okay.

Do your best to turn off as many distractions as possible. Work your way up to no devices and no work.

My favorite meals were on the streets of Spain or on a balcony in Jordan. Soaking up some sunshine, slowly savoring each bite, and quietly enjoying the landscape.

Even when I'm far away from those special places, I try to recreate the feeling and the mindfulness. It never fails to disappoint.

Do I succeed at every meal? Of course not!

Mindful eating isn't about perfection. It's about cultivating awareness one bite at a time.

Closing Thoughts

This small adjustment of slowing to enjoy a meal is transformative, as we've discussed.

As we move forward, remember that eating is more than a biological necessity; it's a celebration of nourishment.

Let's keep learning about additional ways to infuse mindfulness into various aspects of our lives.

Meanwhile, we'll embrace the joy in each bite, and cultivate a mindful approach to nourishing our bodies and souls.

CHAPTER 9: THE MIRROR OF MINDFUL REFLECTION

Taking a moment to pause and reflect might seem like a luxury. However, it's more powerful than we might imagine.

In this chapter, we'll look into mindful reflection—a practice that acts as a mirror, allowing you to see yourself more clearly and navigate the journey of personal and professional growth.

Reflection in Mindfulness

Reflection is the silent partner of mindfulness, offering a space to ponder, understand, and learn from our experiences.

Like the stillness of a pond that allows the water to settle, reflection reveals a new image of our surroundings.

Self-Awareness

Key to unlocking self-awareness—an understanding of your thoughts, emotions, and actions—is mindful reflection.

It's like being handed a map of your internal landscape,

helping you navigate the terrains of your mind.

Benefits of Regular Reflection in a Professional Context

In the professional realm, reflection is a compass, guiding you towards growth and success.

Consider a work project as a journey. Reflecting on its challenges and successes is like a compass that helps you navigate future endeavors more skillfully.

As we've seen in previous chapters, practical application of mindfulness principles yields results in many very practical ways. Mindful reflection is no different.

Improved Decision-Making: Reflection provides insights gained from past decisions, helping you make wiser choices as you move forward.

Enhanced Problem-Solving: The fresh and broader perspective attained from reflecting on a problem enables the implementation of creative solutions.

Daily Mindful Review

Rest assured, making reflection a consistent part of your routine does not require hours of silent contemplation. Carving out a few intentional moments is sufficient.

Structured Reflection Exercises for Personal and Professional Growth

Gratitude Reflection: Take a few moments to consider some of your entries in your gratitude journal from chapter four. Consider why you're grateful for them and how they came about.

Challenge Reflection: Consider a difficulty you faced, explore what created the challenge, how you faced it, and what tactics you would repeat or edit in the future.

Achievement Reflection: Acknowledge a success, recognizing the efforts that led to it and the benefits you've derived since then.

Making Reflection a Consistent Habit

Start by dedicating five minutes at the end of each day to reflect. As it becomes a natural part of your routine, you may choose to expand the time.

This is similar to the balance of watering a plant. Regular, small doses lead to growth. Consistency is the key to reaping the benefits of mindful reflection.

Closing Thoughts

In the album of mindful practices, reflection is the photo that captures the essence of your journey.

As our journey nears its end, remember that reflection isn't about dwelling on the past. Although we do examine the past, reflection is actually a forward-looking tool for growth.

Our last chapter will help us create rituals based on everything we learned thus far.

So, let's embrace the mirror of mindful reflection, learn from the reflections it provides, and journey towards a deeper understanding of ourselves and the paths we tread.

CHAPTER 10: CRAFTING YOUR OWN MINDFUL RITUALS

Rituals are the sounds of the bass shaping the symphony of life.

It's time for us to prepare mindful rituals—a practice that capitalizes on routines to generate the greatest investment.

Are you ready to learn the art of creating mindful rituals, the profound significance they hold, and how consistency can turn them into the foundation of a mindful lifestyle?

Creating Mindful Rituals

Mindful rituals bring rhythm and harmony to the symphony of our lives.

These rituals create a stable bass rhythm that frees up space for a more expressive range of notes, turning the ordinary into the extraordinary.

Rituals anchor us in the present moment, offering a sanctuary of intention and awareness.

Think of a ritual as a lighthouse. In the vast sea of daily activities, it guides you back to the shores of mindfulness.

Cultivating Presence: Rituals create pockets of focused attention, allowing you to be fully present.

Building Connection: Shared rituals strengthen bonds, fostering a sense of community and belonging.

Consistency in Building a Mindful Lifestyle

The bass notes by themselves are not particularly exciting but take them out of your favorite upbeat song and ... well, it just won't be the same.

Establishing Habits: Consistent rituals become effortless habits intuitively performed throughout your day.

Stress Reduction: Knowing that certain moments are reserved for mindful rituals brings a sense of predictability, reducing stress.

Morning Mindfulness Ritual

Each morning is like a blank canvas, ready to be painted with a masterpiece. Designing a personalized morning routine sets the tone for your entire day.

Wake Mindfully: Instead of reaching for your phone immediately, take a few moments to welcome the day. Capitalize on the power of brainwave states and decide here who you'll be today.

Mindful Breathing: Incorporate a few deep breaths to center yourself. Oxygenate your brain before you caffeinate it.

Gratitude Practice: Morning is another great option for using the gratitude journal from chapter four. Program your mind to look for solutions, successes, and satisfaction from the start.

Mindful Movement: Taking a few moments to focus on a few favorite stretches can have quite an impact. Let go of tension and start the day strong.

If you're not a morning person or have a tight schedule, don't worry. You don't need a lot of time or even enthusiasm.

A mindful moment can be layered over tasks like enjoying your morning coffee or tea, showering, or even brushing your teeth.

It's easy to formulate a ritual to suit your needs. Personally, I keep both a mental and paper list of what benefits me most in the mornings.

Each night, when I briefly review "today and tomorrow", I craft the timing and elements of the next morning's routine.

It's become such a habit, I don't do it consciously very often. It never takes more than two minutes.

The beauty of mindful rituals lies in their flexibility. Freely tailor the rituals to suit your preferences and needs. The ritual can change as often as you need.

Closing Thoughts

Many of the world's most successful business leaders are known to have a variety of rituals. That's because they work.

As we conclude this journey, remember that rituals aren't rigid routines; they are dynamic expressions of your mindfulness.

Before we do a brief review and tie everything together, I invite you to consider what you've gleaned from this book and what you most want to apply.

Will your main points be in the conclusion? Keep an eye out for anything you may have completely dismissed.

Perhaps you have already mastered it. Perhaps that's the most difficult practice for you. Either way, these are the practices we tend to overlook or avoid but that we often benefit from the most.

If you need to take a few days to craft and implement your morning ritual or an evening one, I hope you'll give yourself permission to do so.

When you're ready, move on to the conclusion.

CONCLUSION

Nurturing Mindfulness in Your Busy World

As we draw the curtain on this journey through mindfulness for busy professionals, let's take a moment to reflect on the key practices that can transform the chaos of your daily life into a mindful symphony. These simple yet profound practices are like seeds planted in the fertile soil of your routines, ready to bloom into a garden of well-being.

Recap of Key Practices

Breath Awareness: The simple act of tuning into your breath, your anchor in the present moment, brings immediate calmness.

Mindful Micro-Breaks: Recognizing the need for short pauses throughout your day can rejuvenate your mind and enhance productivity.

Mindful Gratitude: Cultivating gratitude in daily life shifts your focus to the positive, fostering emotional well-being.

Mindful Technology Use: Becoming aware of your relationship with technology allows you to harness its benefits without succumbing to its pitfalls.

Mindful Movement: Incorporating simple movements into your day isn't just about physical health; it's a dance that connects your body and mind.

Mindful Listening: Actively engaging in conversations, truly hearing the words and emotions, deepens your connections with others.

Mindful Eating: Savoring each bite turns meals into moments of joy, nurturing both your body and soul.

Mindful Reflection: The silent partner of mindfulness, reflection, offers a mirror to understand, learn, and grow from your experiences.

Mindful Rituals: Creating intentional moments in your day transforms routines into sacred ceremonies, fostering presence and connection.

Morning Mindfulness Ritual: Crafting a personalized morning routine sets the tone for a mindful day, embracing intention and gratitude.

The Cumulative Impact

Individually, these practices are like single notes, but together, they compose a symphony of well-being.

The breath you take during a mindful pause harmonizes with the gratitude you express, creating a melody that echoes throughout your day.

It's not about perfection but about the cumulative impact of weaving mindfulness into the rituals of your life.

As you implement these techniques into your busy life , remember that mindfulness is a versatile companion, adaptable to the ebb and flow of your schedule. It's not an additional burden but a toolkit that empowers you to navigate the demands of your life with grace and resilience.

Utilize to the full the flexibility these practices offer. Experiment, adapt, and find what resonates with you.

Mindfulness is not another rigid set of rules; it's a dynamic dance where you lead, and the practices follow.

Whether you find solace in a mindful breath during a hectic meeting or discover joy in a gratitude practice before bedtime, let your journey be uniquely yours.

Embrace Experimentation

Mindfulness is not a final destination but a perpetual exploration. Continue to experiment with these practices, seeking what aligns with your values and enhances your well-being.

In the evolving landscape of your life, let mindfulness be the compass that guides you towards moments of peace, joy, and fulfillment.

What's next?

I would like to sincerely express my gratitude for you. Yes, thank you for purchasing the book. More importantly, thank you for investing time and effort into yourself.

The more you grow and develop into the kind of person who loves and enjoys life, the more you inspire others to do the same. What an amazing gift that is to all of us as a human family!

My hope is that you found some benefit from this book, a new idea or a new perspective on an old one. I would be deeply grateful for a favorable review of the book on Amazon.

If you're looking for some assistance applying any of the principles in the book, I am a trained mind management coach and would be happy to work with you. You can learn more at www.askpaloma.com .

As you close this chapter and embark on the next steps of your mindful journey, may each breath be a reminder of your commitment to well-being. May each mindful moment be a stepping stone towards a more balanced and harmonious life.

Your journey is your own, and the symphony of mindfulness awaits you, ready to play in tune with the rhythm of your unique existence. Go enjoy it!

RESOURCES

American Psychological Association. (2024). APA Topics: Mindfulness. Retrieved from https://www.apa.org/topics/mindfulness

Harvard Gazette. (April 17, 2018). With mindfulness, life's in the moment. Retrieved from https://news.harvard.edu/gazette/

International Mental Health Hotline Directory. (2024). Mental Health Helplines. Retrieved from https://www.helpguide.org/find-help.htm.

Mayo Clinic. (Oct. 11, 2022). Mindfulness exercises. Retrieved from https://www.mayoclinic.org/healthy-lifestyle/consumer-health/in-depth/mindfulness-exercises/art-20046356#:~:text=Mindfulness%20is%20a%20type%20of,mind%20and%20help%20reduce%20stress.

National Institutes of Health. (June 2021). Mindfulness for Your Health. Retrieved from https://newsinhealth.nih.gov/2021/06/mindfulness-your-health

Psychology Today. (2024). Mindfulness. Retrieved from https://www.psychologytoday.com/us/basics/mindfulness

ABOUT THE AUTHOR

J Paloma Litteral

As a world-renowned mind management coach, ESL teacher, and author, Paloma has worked with hundreds of clients from all around the world to discover and reach their amazing potential. She is constantly learning something new; one of her fundamental principles being: Learning is Life.

A unique blend of compassionate understanding, creative problem solving, and pragmatic action plans awaits you with Paloma's one-of-a-kind perspective.

With accredited certifications in a wide variety of techniques and fields, Paloma's developed a creative approach to self-improvement that is personalized to each client.